Write Book
Make Money

Monetize Your Existing Knowledge and Publish a Bestselling eBook

David De Las Morenas

Copyright © 2014 David De Las Morenas

All rights reserved.

ISBN-13: 978-1502384393

ISBN-10: 1502384396

Disclaimer

All attempts have been made to verify the information in this book; however neither the author nor the publisher assumes any responsibility for errors, omissions, or contrary interpretations of the content within.

This book is for entertainment purposes only, and so the views of the author should not be taken as expert instruction or commands. The reader is responsible for his or her own actions.

Adherence to all applicable laws, including but not limited to international, federal, state, and local regulations governing professional licensing, business practices, advertising, and all other aspects of doing business in the United States or any other jurisdiction is the sole responsibility of the purchaser or reader.

Neither the author nor the publisher assumes any responsibility or liability on behalf of the purchaser or reader of this book.

Buyer Bonus

As a way of saying thank you for your purchase, I'm offering a FREE eBook that's exclusive to my book and blog readers.

It's called **How To Beast: The Manual** and it details the top 3 habits men should adopt to drastically improve their confidence, charisma, discipline, and productivity.

Inside you'll learn:

* A Simple Bodyweight Routine to Shred Fat and Build Muscle

* Simple Meditation: 5 Minutes per Day to Rewire Your Brain and Change Your Life

* How to Approach Any Girl and Get Her Number and a Date in Under 60 Seconds

Download it here: **www.HowToBeast.com/free-ebook**

Dedication

Thank you to the beastly followers of HowToBeast.com who gave me the push I needed to finally write a book about my writing process.

And thank you to my brother Antonio, who's always been my mentor in the realm of writing, and who gave this book an impeccable proofing (he better have, at least). Now go write your own book already.

Contents

How An Experiment In Self-Publishing Quickly Turned Into Thousands Of Dollars In My Pocket Every Week **pg.1**

Why Self-Publish An eBook? Why On Amazon? Why Now? **pg.9**

How To Use This Book **pg.13**

Phase 1: How To Discover Your Most Profitable, Marketable Existing Knowledge **pg.15**

Phase 2: A Simple System For Writing Easy-To-Follow, Engaging Books That Sell (without being a "good" writer) **pg.33**

Phase 3: The 5 Things You Must Do Before Publishing To Ensure Maximum Sales **pg.55**

Phase 4: A Step By Step Guide To Formatting, Uploading, And Publishing Your eBook (and cracking the key options that will determine your sales success) **pg.77**

Phase 5: The Secret To Unleashing Amazon's Built-In Marketing Machine To Sell Thousands Of Copies **pg.87**

How To Maintain Sales In The Long Run, Build A Business Around Self-Publishing, And Other Common Questions Answered **pg.97**

Can You Do Me a Favor? **pg.113**

You Might Also Like My New Online Bootcamp **pg.115**

My Other Books **pg.117**

About the Author **pg.119**

How An Experiment In Self-Publishing Quickly Turned Into Thousands Of Dollars In My Pocket Every Week

The Initial Experiment

I had recently begun working my first nine to five career job. I was maybe one year graduated from university.

One day I read an article about self-publishing books. I think it was on James Altucher's blog. He's an incredible entrepreneur and author who's been one of my main mentors over the past few years. As a side note, I highly suggest checking out his blog and books.

Anyway, I decided I wanted to self-publish a book. And it wasn't because I want to make money. Honestly I don't recall exactly why. I couldn't even stand writing papers in school. I was always more of a math and science type of guy.

I just wanted to be able to say that I was a published author, I guess. Yes, I have an ego that needs to be fed from time to time.

I was also in the midst of a self-improvement renaissance... more like an obsession with reading self-help books, actually. And writing was something new to me – a chance to create something of my own. Whatever the reason, I was motivated to do it just for the sake of doing it.

But what was I to write about?

Over the past few years I'd developed another obsession: bodybuilding. I spent my third year of university studying and working abroad in Madrid, where I befriended a work colleague who happened to be an amateur bodybuilder.

His passion for lifting weights and tracking his diet slowly spread to me and, before you know it, I was counting my calories and lifting weights like a madman – trying to get bigger and stronger.

This journey was not an easy one. Like any kid who's picked up a new hobby or obsession, I was expecting instant results. I reasoned that because I was following a respected routine that I'd found on the internet (the internet doesn't lie) and counting my calories (to GAIN weight – I was a skinny bastard) that I would look like the Rock or a young Arnold Schwarzenegger after approximately one summer of hard work. I would walk onto campus and have dudes begging to kiss my toes and girls taking off their soaking wet panties without muttering a single word.

Well, I got to school and my roommates ridiculed me for my obsession, and the hilarious amount of supplements that cluttered our new apartment (guilty as charged).

But this was a couple of years later, after having remained dedicated in the gym and having researched countless scientific journals. I had made some decent progress at this point.

So, as I laid on the floor of my one bedroom Boston apartment, staring at the ceiling and thinking about what my book should be about, I had the realization that I should write a guide book for people who are just getting into lifting weights. I would include dozens of scientific resources to prove that my book wasn't just another hyped up piece of bullshit. And I would explain the basic science behind all of my recommendations, so as to convince people that this was the real deal.

After a couple months of work, I released *The Simple Art of Bodybuilding: A Practical Guide to Training and Nutrition.* After going through the steps to get it active on the Amazon.com kindle store, I made a posting on the Bodybuilding.com forums and emailed some friends and family to check it out. That was the only thing that resembled any sort of *marketing* that I did.

To my complete bewilderment, people were actually buying it. And I was making several hundred dollars per week. So I sat back, enjoyed the extra cash, and forgot about self-publishing... for the time being.

But Then I Came Back For More

Over the next year or so I barely thought about my book. Yes, from time to time I'd mention to people that I was "a published author", but that was about it (it's not a good reason to publish a book – I experienced only a small increase in the amount sex and respect I enjoyed beforehand).

Then I decided to change careers from software to personal training, and so I leveraged the book as a resume builder. I originally had published the book under the code name *David DLM* (yes, super secretive, I know). At this point I decided to change it to my full name so that potential employers could see how *cool* and *legit* I was.

I made the career change successfully and decided I wanted to self-publish again. But this time I would write a far more focused book that would sell like pancakes, or whatever sells really well (very cheap and clean virgin prostitutes, I'd venture to guess).

I wrote *The Book of Bulking: Workouts, Groceries, and Meals for Building Muscle.* This was a departure from *The Simple Art of Bodybuilding's* focus on theory and science. It was a focused diet and workout plan for skinny guys wanting to bulk up, as had been my challenge.

I wrote it in one week. But it flopped, and made almost no money.

I was still determined, however. I decided to write a self-improvement style book, because that's what I loved to read and I thought the last few years of my life could serve as valuable motivation for other people. I'd gone from an insecure college grad working a cubicle job to someone who felt far more confident, had recently worked up the courage to change careers, and revolutionized my dating success and confidence somewhere along the way.

After several months of work, and a couple re-writes, I released *The Book of Alpha: 30 Rules I Followed to Radically Enhance My Confidence, Charisma, Productivity, Success, and Life.*

Success at Last

The response I got was nothing short of unbelievable. Sure, my marketing strategy had vastly improved, and I had opted to release a paperback with the kindle version, but still I was shocked.

I was easily making thousands of dollars each and every week. The book quickly climbed the charts and sat at number one on Amazon's Men Health rankings for a long period of time. And I still wasn't in it for the money. I felt like a true entrepreneur (humble brag).

Since then, I've continued to experiment with my basic methodology, and experienced more and more financial success, in less and less turnaround time. I can easily conceive, write, edit, publish, and successfully market a book in less than one month now.

My book "business" quickly surpassed the income I was making from working for a software company as well as from training my clients in the gym. It remains my main source of income to this day.

It's against Amazon's terms of service to release exactly how much I make, but I assure you that it's several thousands of dollars per week. I've released five books in total (this will be number six). It's regular for the Men's Health bestseller list to look something like this:

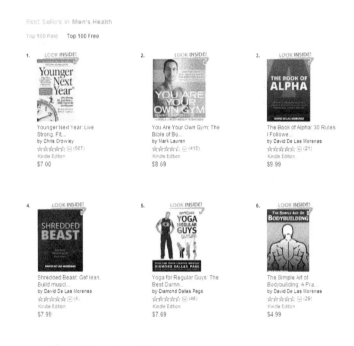

My first three books sitting pretty at numbers 3, 4, and 6 of the Men's Health bestseller list

My aim in this book is to provide you with the exact step-by-step process I follow to determine how to write my next book: what I do to actually write it, how to publish it, and the easiest way to take advantage of Amazon's internal marketing system — this last is the crucial piece of knowledge that will allow you to sells thousands of books and actually turn a profit.

This is a system that I've improved with each book I've published. I believe it will serve as an invaluable resource to anyone who wants to make some good money off of their existing knowledge by writing and publishing a Kindle eBook.

Good luck. Now go make that money.

David

Why Self-Publish An eBook? Why On Amazon? Why Now?

While I stumbled upon self-publishing and eBook wealth through a series of fortunate events, the truth is that there is significant and compelling data that supports my decision.

There is significant data showing that self-publishing an eBook is an extremely plausible way for anyone to turn a profit in today's economy.

Put simply:

The eBook Market Has EXPLODED, And It's Only Getting Bigger

Here are some interesting numbers for you to mull over:

- **30%:** The proportion of all books sold that are eBooks – and this is growing rapidly.

- **65%:** The proportion of eBooks sold that are Amazon Kindle titles – also growing.

- $5.25 billion: Amazon's annual revenue from book sales.

- Greater than 50%: The percent decrease in the number of independent bookstores over the past 20 years.

All of this goes to say that the eBook market is growing fast, and that Amazon has a chokehold on the market. There's a lot of money out there that people are spending on eBooks, and you can easily grab some of it IF you can provide value to these potential customers.

Self-Publishing Is More Profitable Than Getting A Book Deal

My main reason for being a proponent of self-publishing eBooks: it's super easy and you keep most of the profit when you use Kindle to sell your book.

I've begun to also publish my books in paperback format, but they're more challenging to format and they don't turn close to as much profit (I do include some basic instructions for you in the back, though, if you choose to publish a paperback along with your eBook).

Here are some numbers to back me up:

- **70%:** The royalty (share of the profits) that goes to you for every Kindle book you sell (there are a few restrictions here, but I assure you that I get 70% on nearly all of my sales).

- **5-25%:** The royalty that traditionally published authors receive from publishing companies.

Yes, if you somehow manage to get a book deal, you'll get a fat check up front, but in the long run a book that sells well has the potential to make you more if it's self-published. And, honestly, you're probably not about to get a book deal anytime soon anyway.

Another caveat of self-publishing is that you own the rights to your work. When you get a book deal, the publisher takes control of those rights.

But I digress. What you need to see and believe is that self-publishing on Amazon Kindle is a proven way for cool guys like you and I to make some cash.

How To Use This Book

This book is meant to be used as a guide for writing your own eBook AND actually making real profit off of it. It makes sense to actually do the prescribed steps and create your own book as you go along. It's not a fairy tale or an epic novel that's meant to entertain you or serve as some sort of strange pornography (although maybe I should look into that market).

While I do recommend working on your project for as many consecutive days as you can (so as to generate momentum), you don't have to do it in any specific timeframe. Simply pick up this book when you have an hour or so to put towards the next step in creating your own book.

Each phase consists of a series of steps, and each of these is meant to be completed in one sitting (they will take 30 minutes to 1 hour on average). That's all; now go make some money.

Phase 1: How To Discover Your Most Profitable, Marketable Existing Knowledge

Each of us has a unique collection of knowledge and experiences. This is a fact.

And there are people out there who are facing the same problems, challenges, and obstacles that you overcame yesterday, last month, or last year. This is also a fact.

By writing a book and making it available on Amazon, you're doing them a huge favor. You're giving them a solution that they need or want. And this is valuable – they are willing to pay for it.

You may not think you have the "authority" to write a book.

But what even is authority? I assure you that your existing knowledge, with potentially a little bit of extra research, is enough to guide other people to a particular result. You don't need a bunch of letters after your name, or a million other published books in order to achieve this.

You may not think you have the skill.

Writing is simple. You simply put your words on paper. And if you're really skeptical about your writing, it's dirt cheap to hire a copy editor to fix your grammar and "improve" what you've already written. But this is not necessary. I include some tips later on how to make writing easier.

You may think you don't have the time.

An hour or two a day, for four or five days per week is enough to follow all of the steps in this book and produce a quality eBook in about one month's time. Of course, you can do less, but the amount of work you put in will dictate exactly how long it takes you, but anywhere from two weeks to two months is average.

That's my motivational coach speech. I hope you're super excited now.

This section (phase one) is dedicated to walking you through the steps you should follow to determine exactly what to write about.

Step 1: Generate a list of things that you've "figured out"

So, what exactly do you know that people would be willing to pay for? Here's when you think really hard for a while and find the answer to that question.

I want you to brainstorm an exhaustive list of everything that you've "figured out". This could be literally any challenge, problem, issue, or test that you've faced and overcame.

Your task is to create a word document or take out a notebook and write down NO FEWER THAN ten potential ideas. They don't have to be great. They just have to be.

Below are the first fifteen things that came to my mind, use them to get your juices flowing if you're feeling stuck.

1. How I went from super skinny to quickly gaining weight and building muscle

2. How I went from being super shy to being able to approach women during the day and get phone numbers and dates

3. The method I developed to use the Tinder dating mobile application to get dates every night of the week

4. How to overcome intense social anxiety and be able to confidently express yourself

5. How to build and grow a side revenue stream and quit your 9 to 5 job

6. The daily habits I practice to stay confident and motivated during stressful or depressing periods

7. How to use the Evernote application to organize your entire life and radically improve your productivity

8. The simple routine I developed to finally break past the resistance and start meditating every day

9. How I write books and make money on kindle using information I already know

10. A guide to better sex for virgins and relatively inexperienced men

11. A simple guide for new personal trainers to quickly build a clientele and give them intense, appropriate training sessions that will keep them coming back

12. A basic strategy to make money playing online no limit Texas hold 'em

13. A quick guide to prepare you for the MCAT/LSAT/GRE in under X months

14. How I traveled the world with only a backpack and lived for under X dollars per month

15. A guide to Boston's nightlife: the best bars for watching sports, pickup, or going on a date

This list is by no means exhaustive. Some of those things I've already written about, others I will eventually, and others I know absolutely nothing about and will never write about but included anyway.

Write your list before proceeding to the next step.

Step 2: Narrow your list and focus on your "best" choices

When I get that itch to write another book (or realize that it's time to make more money), I start by brainstorming a bunch of potential options, like you just did in step one.

However, most of them aren't things that I can really picture myself sitting at a computer and typing about for extended periods of time without contemplating suicide (or just lots of buffalo chicken calzones).

For example, my latest two books *Shredded Beast* and *Dominate* were completely different writing experiences. When I wrote *Shredded Beast,* a men's fitness book, I wasn't really in a fitness frame of mind. As a result, it seemed like a chore.

However, when I wrote *Dominate,* a book about cultivating a fearless, aggressive mindset towards life, I was so pumped to do the research to find accurate historical examples for each of my points and to explore my own experiences that the book was an immense pleasure to write.

I literally looked forward to the first two hours of every morning when I'd sit down to type the next chapter or two of the book. In fact, I spent so much time writing and thinking about it, that it pissed my girlfriend off. Like really badly.

It's probably no coincidence that we broke up right before I published the book. Um, maybe that's not the sales pitch I wanted to give, but you get the idea: writing a book you're excited about doesn't feel like work – it feels like sex. Well, not quite, but it's pretty damn fulfilling and stimulating.

Your next task is to narrow your list of ten or more potential ideas to just five – the five that sound like they would be the most fun and engaging for you to research and write about.

Before I decided to write this book my list of potential books was:

1. How to monetize your existing knowledge and write a bestselling kindle eBook (this one)

2. 15 confidence hacks to make you feel, look, and act more confident

3. How to use the Tinder application to line up dates for every night of the week

4. Exercise, nutrition, posture, and style tips for skinny guys to create a dominant presence

5. How I went from being super shy to being able to approach women during the day and get phone numbers and dates

Step 3: Analyze your short list and identify the most profitable ideas

There's a saying: *if a tree falls down in the forest and nobody sees it, did it really fall down?*

Don't think about that too hard.

When applied to your eBook, this saying means: if you write a book and nobody reads it, does it even matter that you wrote the book?

The point I'm making is that you want to be sure that an audience exists for your book. This way people will buy it, read it, and review it. And you'll receive a large amount of green paper (or whatever color your money or bitcoins are). The question is HOW do you verify if such an audience exists?

Task one is to take each of your five potential ideas and describe the type of person who would buy a book about that topic – the type of person you were before solving that particular problem.

For example, using my choices from step 2:

1. How to monetize your existing knowledge and write a bestselling kindle eBook (this one)

People with an entrepreneurial inclination who are looking for a new business venture

2. 15 confidence hacks to make you feel, look, and act more confident

Pretty much any guy who reads self-help type books

3. How to use the Tinder application to line up dates for every night of the week

Any guy who uses, or is intrigued by, the Tinder dating app

4. Exercise, nutrition, posture, and style tips for skinny guys to create a dominant presence

Skinny guys who think that they come off as insecure who read self-help type books

5. How I went from being super shy to being able to approach women during the day and get phone numbers and dates

Guys who are interested in meeting women and want to do it outside of bars and clubs

Next, see if you can cross one or two options off the list based just on this information. Anything that is super general is a good candidate for throwing away.

In my case, numbers 1 and 2 are very general, so I would scrap those.

Note: Yes, I know, I am writing about option 1 right now, but that's because I polled my blog's email list to see what they wanted. If you have access to a large email list of potential buyers then yes, you can use that as a tool here.

Now, hopefully you have just three options left. They should all seem like they'd be fun to write and pertain to at least semi-specific audiences.

The last way you can eliminate potentially poor choices is by testing your keywords with Amazon's search suggestions, because it suggests terms to finish your search that are commonly searched for.

Your last task for this step is to type in several probable searches for each of your remaining three or four titles. Think about what someone looking for a solution to their problem would search for and then type it into Amazon.com's search box. If Amazon auto-fills in something that is relevant to your idea before you finish it, then that means people are looking for it.

For example, my Tinder dating idea:

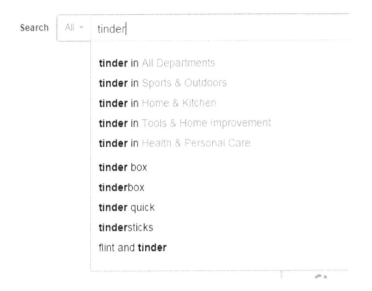

All of the top searches that show up when I type "Tinder" have nothing to do with the dating app. This is a bad sign of potential interest.

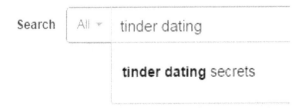

If I add the word "dating" to my search, I get just one relevant suggestion: "tinder dating secrets". Not terrible, but you can do a lot better.

Let's stick with the dating niche and explore my other idea – how to meet women during the daytime.

I start with the very broad search "how to meet women" and we can see that "how to meet women in public" is something that Amazon suggests. This is a good sign.

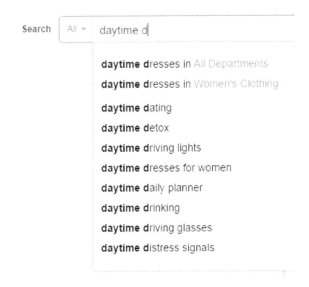

Next, I test to see if "daytime dating" might be suggested when I type just "daytime d" and as you can see, it is.

Based on these brief tests, I would go with the daytime dating book over tinder dating. There is a lot of wiggle room here, and you just have to play around with basic search terms to see which of your ideas seems to have a lot of relevant searches being performed on Amazon. This isn't an exact science, but rather more of an educated guess type of research.

You could certainly use more advanced techniques like Google AdWords to test interest, but that's outside the scope of this book. I want to make this process as simple as possible and I personally don't do anything more than this simple testing, so I'll leave it at that.

Step 4: Create a working title and begin your new journey

Now that you've done some basic research and analysis on your top five choices, it's time to pick one.

Don't get overly obsessed here – if step 3 didn't give you a clear choice then just go with your gut and choose the idea that you want to write the most.

This guarantees you'll enjoy the process, and if it passed the tests in step 3 then it definitely has at least some marketability.

You can always write another book after this one. And at the very least, you will learn a few invaluable skills by writing, publishing, and marketing your book. And most likely earn some cash, too.

Your task is to pick one of your remaining choices and create a working title for it. You will test this later as well, but it's motivating to have something to work towards. Your title should consist of (a) a CATCHY title and (b) a subtitle that states the MAIN BENEFIT.

For example, my working title for this book is "Easy Money: How to Monetize Your Existing Knowledge and Write a Bestselling Kindle eBook". It might have changed by the time you buy it, but that's what it is now.

Phase 2: A Simple System For Writing Easy-To-Follow, Engaging Books That Sell (without being a "good" writer)

"**Vision without action is a dream.** Action without vision is simply passing the time. Action with Vision is making a positive difference."

- David Allen, author of *Getting Things Done* (read this book ASAP)

The bolded part of this quote is what I want you to focus on. By completing phase 1, you've already created your **vision** – a book that you want to write, based on your existing knowledge and experiences.

However, without **action**, this does you no good. It does your potential readers no good.

Writing can be tough. And writing an entire book can seem impossible. It usually does for me, even after having written a handful.

But I've created a system that makes writing a complete book inevitable and enjoyable. Phase 2 is dedicated to taking you through this system, step by step.

This system is designed for people who don't write a lot. It's designed to break up the writing process into small, manageable chunks that can be completed, one day at a time. This keeps me sane and motivated.

More importantly, it's a system that produces non-fiction guide-type books that are super easy to understand and implement all while being entertaining reads. There's nothing worse than having to put a book down because it's too hard to follow or because it's just too damn boring.

Follow these steps and you will avoid these common pitfalls and create a book that's built to sell.

Step 1: Break down your unique process and turn it into a polished system

The key to making learning a new concept digestible is breaking it down into smaller steps.

If I were to write this book without phases or steps, it would be a disaster.

Not only do smaller steps make something easier to learn, they also make it *seem* less intimidating, give the reader a sense of progress as they make their way through your work, and give *you* a sense of progress as you write your work.

And perhaps most importantly: they allow you to organize your thoughts and refine your existing knowledge.

Before I wrote this book, I intuitively knew how to monetize things I'd figured out, and package them as books that would sell. However, I wouldn't have been able to, off the top of my head, describe to you an easy-to-follow process that would make sense.

Instead I would probably have rambled on about how you'd already know something that'd be valuable to others, and then switched to rambling about Amazon's marketing system (which you'll learn about later) and how it's actually pretty easy to take advantage of. Then I might have gone in reverse and talked about my writing process a bit. Then I might have started talking about this one girl that I'm dating and how she's the opposite of the last. Then I might have started talking about my latest adventure, riding ATVs in the Sahara Desert…

You would be completely confused, and probably question my intelligence and mental well-being – as well as your ability to ever write a book.

By taking the time to really think about the steps that you follow, and exactly the order in which you follow them, you'll create something invaluable: your own unique system for accomplishing a particular outcome.

Not only this, but in the process of creating this system, you'll actually refine the system itself, and your final product will actually end up better than what you begin with.

I'm saying that what you're getting in this book is actually an improved version of the workflow I've followed in the past to create and write books, AND that next time I write a book, I will do it a bit more efficiently, because the process of defining my workflow has forever improved it.

Your task is to break down the process you follow to achieve the solution you're providing into a series of larger steps. Five to ten is a good number to shoot for.

For example, for this book my initial steps (that became the overarching phases of this book) were:

1. Figure out something valuable you know to write about

2. Write the book itself

3. Edit it and include a few keys things

4. Format it, upload it, give it keywords, and price it

5. Getting initial sales that will create momentum inside of Amazon

To give you another example, my book about how to meet girls on Tinder would have looked something like this:

1. Set up your profile and take quality pictures

2. An efficient swiping strategy

3. Send a good first message

4. Conduct basic small talk

5. Close and get her number

6. Text her to set up a date

7. Go on the date and focus on these things

NOTE: You don't have to create a step-by-step process – my book *The Book of Alpha* for example was a collection or list of rules to follow in order to achieve more confidence. The important thing is that you break your idea up into distinct pieces of information that can be consumed separately.

Even my latest fitness book *Shredded Beast* was a collection of chapters, some instructional and others purely informational. The point is that you must divide the information up in some way that makes logical sense and is easy to follow.

Step 2: Edit your process to make it "sales-ready"

Now that you have your steps, I want you to refine their wording. Yes, really.

This may seems silly but it gets you to focus on delivering a solution that focuses on the benefits, not the process. AND people buy things because they want to achieve a particular set of benefits, NOT because they want to do the steps necessary to getting there.

This will also serve to create a solid table of contents that gets potential buyers interested when they preview your book (and you can also use your table of contents in your book blurb to convey a lot of value).

Your task is to re-word your steps so that they convey the benefits of completing that step, not the process of doing the step itself.

For example, my initial steps from step 1 were:

1. Figure out something valuable you know to write about

2. Write the book itself

3. Edit it and include a few keys things

4. Format it, upload it, give it keywords, and price it

5. Getting initial sales that will create momentum inside of Amazon

And I changed them to:

*Phase 1: How To Discover Your Most **Profitable**, Marketable Existing Knowledge*

*Phase 2: A Simple System For Writing Easy-To-Follow, Engaging **Books That Sell** (without being a writer)*

*Phase 3: The 5 Things You Must Do Before Publishing To **Ensure Maximum Sales***

Phase 4: A Step By Step Guide To Formatting, Uploading, Pricing, And Publishing Your eBook

*Phase 5: The Secret To Unleashing Amazon's Built-In Marketing Machine To **Sell Thousands Of Copies***

As you can see the majority of these new items focus around the idea that each step will ensure that you create a book that **makes you money** (I've bolded some of the key words above).

This is the reason that people will buy my book. Yes, maybe a few potential buyers will just want to write a book for the sake of publishing their own books, but most people will buy it because they actually want to make more money.

For my dating book, I would've chose words that focused around dates, sex, and girlfriends – the obvious benefits that anyone who uses a dating app wants to achieve.

Figure out what the benefits that someone who's buying your book is after, and then structure your steps' wording around them.

Step 3: Create a detailed roadmap to swiftly guide you to a finished product

I'll be honest: creating an outline is probably the toughest step in writing a book. Not the most time consuming – no, writing takes longer for sure – but the most challenging.

You want to create an outline that is detailed enough so that when you sit down to write, you can be in autopilot mode the entire time. You want to create an outline that defines each of your steps in detail, and includes any anecdotes or supporting examples from your life – or other people's lives, for that matter.

If you weren't to create an outline, and instead just sat down at your laptop hoping to save some time and pull a quick bestseller out of your ass, you would be stupid. Or really damn smart. But chances are that you'd write for a few minutes and then realize you didn't know what direction you were going in. Then you'd give up altogether and scream "fuck this whole eBook thing anyway, I'll just eat some pop tarts and jerk off instead" (I might be projecting).

Bite the bullet up front, spend an hour or so putting together a quality outline, and then breeze through the rest of the writing process.

Here are your guidelines:

- The introduction should be your story, and it should be detailed and include all of the obstacles and challenges you faced and then overcame along your journey. This is meant to create a connection with the reader and build plausibility in his mind that he too can accomplish what you have.

- After the intro you can jump right into the method, or include a couple sections of further introduction (i.e. *how to read and follow this book* or *why Tinder is a goldmine for meeting attractive women* or even *some interesting facts and figures about self-published books*).

- Next is the method itself. Each of your primary steps will be its own chapter. Include as many examples from your own life, your friends' lives, or the lives of notable people as you can to support your method. This adds evidence to make your claims more believable, and more importantly, makes your book fun and engaging to read. People love stories, and it's what will make your book unique among similar guides.

- Finish with a brief conclusion that recaps the process in a few pages if it makes sense. This should be a reference for a reader to look at for a quick refresher or dose of motivation after having read the book.

For example, this book's initial outline looked something like this (chapter headings in bold):

How An Experiment In Self-Publishing Quickly Turned Into Thousands Of Dollars In My Pocket Every Week (MY STORY)

Some Interesting Numbers About Self-Publishing Versus Traditional Publishing (FURTHER INTRODUCTION)

Phase 1: How To Discover Your Most Profitable, Marketable Knowledge (BEGIN THE METHOD)

- Step 1: List everything you've figured out

- Step 2: Narrow your options

- Step 3: Discover which have most potential

- Step 4: Pick one

Phase 2: A Simplified System For Writing Easy-To-Follow, Engaging Books That Sell (without being a writer)

- Step 1: Break down the process

- Step 2: Refine the steps

- Step 3: Create the outline

- Step 4: Prepare a word document

- Step 5: The writing process

… Phases 3-5 (THE REST OF THE METHOD)

How To Maintain Sales In The Long Run, Build A Business Around Self-Publishing, And Other Common Questions (CONCLUSION)

No, I didn't include my entire outline here, but up through phase 2 that's exactly what I used. The four or five sub-steps per chapter were enough for me to sit down and write an entire chapter per day without having to think much.

Your sub-steps should do the same for you. Whether you need two, five, ten, or twenty sub-steps to accomplish this… That's up to you.

You'll notice I didn't include specific stories or examples in my outline. This is because this book itself is used as a running example throughout. I suggest including at least a few stories per chapter to avoid coming across like an instruction manual for an old television set.

Step 4: Prepare your Word document correctly to avoid wasted time when you publish the book later

NOTE: I use Microsoft Word as an example for creating your eBook throughout this book. If you don't have Word, then you can use any software that allows you to format your document as I instruct (page breaks, heading styles, saving as HTML file, etc.). I recommend Microsoft Office Starter or Open Office (both are free downloads).

This chapter will be purely instructional, but it should only take you 10 minutes. Setting up your Word document correctly right now will make uploading your book to Amazon Kindle super easy later on.

The first book I published was a nightmare. I spent hours upon hours trying to figure out a format that worked.

Follow these five steps and when you have to finalize your book for upload it will only take a few minutes.

Note: This is definitely not the ONLY way to do this, but it is the way that I use and it works well.

1. Create a new word document

2. Title page: Using the default font (Word calls it *Normal*), type your title (bolded), subtitle (italicized), and author name all on separate lines at the top of the first page and center them like so:

Easy Money

How to Monetize Your Existing Knowledge and Publish Your First Bestselling eBook

David De Las Morenas

3. Copyright page: Click **CTRL+ENTER** (on PC) or **APPLE+ENTER** (on Mac) to create a page break and advance to a new page (**NOTE:** You must use a page break in between every page that should be viewed as a separate page by Kindle). Using the default font again, type the following text and center it:

Copyright © 2014 David De Las Morenas

All rights reserved.

Replace my name with yours or the company's name that will hold the book's copyright. This is enough to protect you and your work from plagiarism and copying.

4. Create another page break and change your font to *Heading 1*, and type in your first chapter's name. Click **ENTER** to advance one line and change the font back to *Normal* before you begin typing your introductory chapter.

NOTE: You must repeat step 4 and include a page break every time you create a new chapter. We will cover how to include a table of contents later, when you're done with the book.

5. Save your work. Do it often and back it up to something like Dropbox in case of hard drive failure.

Step 5: Define and commit to a writing schedule in order to eliminate writers block and crank out your book in no time

I've never been much of a writer. All the way through school I did what I could to get out of writing papers, and cranked things out as fast as humanly possible when I had to. So it still shocks me that I've published a handful of books. It also shocks everyone I know. Friends and family often think I'm making a weird joke when they find out.

The first two were very short. One was about 70 pages and the second was about 40. And while they weren't my most profitable books, they did sell.

However over time I realized that my inability to author a book over 100 pages was limiting my potential. While it's appropriate for some books to be very short, some ideas simply need more than 100 pages of content, examples, and analysis in order to be a valuable asset.

And unfortunately, some people don't take super short books too seriously. Less than 75 or 100 pages starts to seem more like a long blog post than a book worth paying for.

So I slowly figured out why writing longer books was beyond my reach: I was simply afraid of spending so much time on a single project. I have some ADD when it comes to this type of thing, and putting down 100 pages worth of my thoughts and words seemed like it would take an eternity.

Obviously it does take longer than writing 40 pages, but it isn't so bad if you follow two simple rules:

1. Define a sufficient amount of content in your outline

2. Create and commit to a specific writing schedule that you will follow until the book is complete.

You've already tackled step 1. Don't be afraid to go back and add to your outline if you think there is more useful information you can include. You can also subtract anything that seems unnecessary from it.

But step 2 is what you will complete now. Having a writing schedule is magical:

- It turns your book project into a job of sorts that you must show up for until it's complete

- It allows you to focus completely on your writing while you're doing it, and then deal with the rest of your life without being distracted by your new project

- It addresses the common protest that "I don't have time" right up front

- And, most importantly, it rapidly increases the chance of you actually finishing your book and cashing in on it

Your task is to create a writing schedule that you will adhere to until the book is complete. It should include the times of day and days of the week you will sit down and write, without being distracted by anything else.

I'm writing this book while on a vacation of several weeks in Spain, so my schedule is supremely flexible. I also want to get it done before I leave so it is a bit intense.

If you work a 9-5 job, you will obviously need to work around that, and potentially miss out on some of your regular activities or sleep in order to make time. But realize that the writing process won't take you that long if you stick to a strict schedule.

Mine is: Monday through Friday, 11AM-12PM and 3PM-5PM.

Again, that's probably more time than you have, but yours could easily look something like: Monday through Thursday, 7PM-9PM and Saturday and Sunday, 2PM-5PM.

I don't recommend setting aside less than an hour or more than three at a time. Anything less isn't enough to get into a groove, and anything more will compromise your productivity and mental sanity.

Step 6: Write your book using these two tips to make your book engaging and coherent

I've already said it a bunch of times, but I still don't see myself as a writer. I'm more like a scientist that figured out a formula to produce books.

Along my journey there have been two simple tips that have revolutionized my ability to write some quality shit.

Start writing your book. Follow these two steps each day as you write, and I promise they will make your writing easier and, more importantly, better:

1. Write as if you were talking to a close friend. This makes it easier to get words on paper and actually makes it way more engaging of a read, too.

2. After writing each day, re-read what you have written twice, once editing it for grammar and a second time editing it for content – this means making sure that it makes sense AND ALSO that there is some humor and edginess to it so that it doesn't suck to read.

Now you can put this book down for a while. Your next week or three will be spent actually writing the damn thing. Come back when you're finished.

Write Book, Make Money

Phase 3: The 5 Things You Must Do Before Publishing To Ensure Maximum Sales

At this point, you've written your book. Well, at least a rough draft. And it should be more refined than a first draft if you edited it as you went along.

Congratulations, at this point it's almost certain that you'll finish this project. In a short amount of time you will be a published author (or have published another book if you've already done so). You'll also have a new source of income

However, there's still work to be done. So don't pop that bottle or finance that new Benz quite yet.

This section is dedicated to transforming your draft into a product that's ready for publishing. Once you've completed the following steps, you'll have a final draft, a sleek book cover, an optimized title, and some additional key pages in your book.

For me, this is the most enjoyable part of the process, because your finalized product comes together here. It goes from some words in a Word document to a fresh eBook that's ready to sell.

The feeling that comes with creating something, for me, is one of the best parts of this process. It's both motivating and fulfilling, because you prove to yourself that you're able to step outside of your comfort zone and produce a marketable product.

Step 1: Proof and edit the book to turn it into a polished product

When you buy a book and catch a spelling or grammar error, you feel proud – like you spotted something that the editor missed. If you buy a book and notice four or five errors, it begins to devalue the book. It makes it feel like an amateur piece of work.

And people will subtract stars from their reviews when they see this. Trust me – I've received one or two star reviews that cited a few grammar mistakes as the sole reason for the poor rating. This may seem silly or unreasonable, but some people place a lot of importance on perfection in this area when it comes to published works.

Poor reviews will hurt your visibility within Amazon's internal marketing system, meaning less people will see your book. And people who do see it will be less inclined to purchase it. All of this translates to fewer sales and fewer dollars in your pocket.

So you absolutely MUST proof the book.

I suggest hiring someone (you can find copy-editors quite cheap on eLance.com). It won't cost much, and it will increase the value of your book. Plus you can write it off as a business expense (more on this at the end of the book, but self-published income from Amazon must be reported as self-employment income, and so while it will make your taxes a bit more complicated, you get to report your expenses).

You can also proof the book yourself (see below for my suggestions on how to do this).

Your first task (whether you hire someone or not) is to read through the book from beginning to end. I want you to read it at a normal pace and pay attention to the content:

- Should anything be added to further explain a particular concept?

- Should anything be deleted that's just filler and doesn't add anything to the book?

- Should anything be reorganized or reordered to make the book more coherent?

Your next task is to proof the book. Either hire someone (a friend who has a knack for this or a free-lancer on eLance.com) or do it yourself.

- If you hire someone, read it over after they give it back just to make sure they weren't mentally challenged.

- If you do it yourself, I recommend reading through the book slowly AND out loud. Do this AT LEAST three times through. Do it again if you're still catching errors after your third read-through.

Yes, this part sucks, but it is absolutely required if you give a shit about what you're about to release. Trust me, I've made the mistake of rushing a book out, and it's both embarrassing and unprofessional to have your readers email you corrections to your own book.

NOTE: My brother is a skilled proof reader who does a good job for me. If you'd like to use his services, contact me through my website and I can connect you with him.

Step 2: Add in a few key pages to complete the book and enhance your sales

Over time I've figured out several key pages that should be included in every book I publish. Not including them is shooting myself in the foot and crippling my potential future sales.

Learn from my mistakes and include any of the following pages that are applicable to you and your book. It will make a big difference in your short and long term sales potential.

1. Table of contents

This is straightforward, but here's how you have to do it for Kindle to recognize it and make it so that people can click the chapter titles to navigate directly to the chapters:

1. Create a new page after your copyright page, but before the start of your book (remember to use a page break). Write **Contents** at the top of the page using font *heading 1* and press return to move down one line.

2. Use Word's built in table of contents feature by clicking **References>Table of Contents>Insert Table of Contents**

3. Uncheck **show page numbers** and set **show levels** to 1, then click **OK.**

*You'll need to **right click>update** if you add, delete, or edit any of your headings after this point in order to reflect the changes.

EXTRA STEPS: Now's a good time to bookmark the beginning of your book and the table of contents. Amazon uses these locations to direct readers to the appropriate parts of your book after purchasing.

1. Click right before the title of your book (or further in – wherever you want it to open to when people buy it).

2. Click **Insert>Bookmark** then type in **Start** and click **Add**.

3. Click right before your table of contents heading.

4. Click **Insert>Bookmark** then type in **ToC** and click **Add**.

2. Call to action for reviews

Amazon is more likely to advertise your book to potential buyers if your sales are good and you've accumulated quality reviews. People are also far more willing to buy books with lots of good reviews. So you should ask your readers to leave a review at the end of your book. Here's how:

1. At the end of your book, after your conclusion, create a new page (using a page break, as always). Write **Can You Do Me A Favor?** or something similar at the top using font *heading 1*.

2. Write some text requesting that your readers leave you a review on Amazon. Here's what you'll find at the end of this book:

Thank you for buying and reading my book. I'm confident that you're well on your way to making good money off of your existing knowledge if you simply follow the steps I've laid out here.

Before you go, I have a small favor to ask. Would you take a minute to write a brief blurb about this book on Amazon? Reviews are the best way for independent authors (like me) to get noticed and sell more books. I also read every review and use the feedback to write future revisions – and future books, even.

3. About the author

People want to know about you. You don't have to give them a lot of information. If you included sufficient examples throughout the book then they should already feel a connection, but you should still include an author's page at the end.

1. Make a new page (use a page break) after your *request for reviews* page and write **About the Author** using *heading 1* as your title.

2. Write some text about yourself here. It can be whatever you want. My only recommendation is that you create a sense of authority and include your blog or website, if you have one. Here's what you'll find at the end of this book:

David De Las Morenas is an engineer, personal trainer, and internet entrepreneur known for his bestselling books on men's health and entrepreneurship.

*You can follow him at: **www.HowToBeast.com.***

4. (Optional) Call to action to subscribe to your email list

Building an email list is probably the best thing you can do if you want to build a following of people who will buy, read, and review future books or products you release.

While I won't provide you with a detailed email marketing strategy (that's beyond the scope of this book), at the very least you can email your list when you release a new book and get a small amount of initial sales and reviews.

If you have a blog, this is 100% required. If not, you should still use an email list to collect the emails of buyers of your Amazon books (who are likely to buy future books).

1. Setup an account with a company like *MailChimp* or *Aweber* so that you can build an email list.

2. Use whichever email service you choose to generate a link where people can subscribe to your list.

3. At the beginning of your book, right after the table of contents, create a new page, and give it a heading like **Buyer Bonus** or something similar.

4. Write some text that tells the reader why he should subscribe. At the beginning of this book, I describe the free eBook that I send to new subscribers to my list. If you provide something similar, do the same. If you don't have a free eBook that you give your new subscribers then I'd simply write something like:

As a way of saying thank you for your purchase, I want to offer you the chance to join my EXCLUSIVE email list. By joining you will receive email alerts when I release new books, and you'll have to chance to get ALL of these new releases for just 99 cents!

(More on the 99 cent thing later)

5. Include a link where they can subscribe.

5. (Optional) Call to action to buy another product

If you offer a product on your blog or website that pertains to readers of your new book, then you should include a page at the end of your book detailing it and providing a link for them to get more information about it.

People that just bought and read your eBook are likely to buy another product from you – don't miss out on this opportunity.

6. (Optional) Your other published books

Similar to above, if you've published other books, then include a page at the end of your book that lists your others books. If people like your book, then they're likely to buy others, too.

NOTE: Remember to update your table of contents after adding any of these pages

Step 3: Test your title to ensure maximum "click-ability"

When someone is browsing Amazon, they're constantly bombarded with hundreds of potential links and products to click on. You want to make sure that when your book appears in someone's search results, or elsewhere, it really stands out. People can't buy the book if they don't click on it.

The two parts to dealing with this obstacle are creating a good title and creating a good cover image (more on this in the next step).

Now, as I told you in the first part of this book, I believe the keys to an effective title are a CATCHY title and a subtitle that conveys the main BENEFITS of your book. Here are my most recent titles to demonstrate what I mean by this:

1. Dominate: Conquer your fears. Become the man you want to be.

2. Shredded Beast: Get lean. Build muscle. Be a man.

3. The Book of Alpha: 30 Rules I Followed to Radically Enhance My Confidence, Charisma, Productivity, Success, and Life

Out of these three books, *The Book of Alpha* sells best by far. And I'm pretty sure it's because of the title. It's catchy and the subtitle lists a number of benefits that any man would be crazy not to want.

I'd like to note that it's also the only title that I did NOT test (using Facebook ads) out of the three. I did ask close peers and family members for feedback on that title, however.

Your task is to create roughly three potential titles and then "test" them by asking for people's opinions or by using Facebook Ads.

To test them using Facebook Ads, simply create an ad campaign on Facebook that includes the same exact image for each ad, but has different wording. Whichever ad gets the most clicks wins. I'm not going to go into detail about exactly how to do this, but Facebook makes it pretty straightforward to accomplish.

This gives you're a larger pool of people against whom to test your titles than if you'd just asked friends, but it also costs money (again, this can be cited as an expense on your taxes) and takes a bit of time to do.

Here are the three titles that I'm testing for this book right now (I'm using Facebook Ads):

*1. **Easy Money**: How To Monetize Your Existing Knowledge And Publish A Bestselling eBook*

*2. **Simple Entrepreneurship**: How To Monetize Your Existing Knowledge And Publish A Bestselling eBook*

*3. **Write Book, Make Money**: How To Monetize Your Existing Knowledge And Publish A Bestselling eBook*

NOTE: As you can see, I'm using the same subtitle for each title. This way, there's only one variable that I'm testing at a time. If I want to test the subtitle, I would do this after having selected a title with a new set of Facebook ads.

Otherwise just ask a bunch of friends and family members for their input. I suggest emailing them a list of the potential titles and asking them to tell you which one stands out after only a quick glance.

Step 4: Create a sleek cover image that will attract buyers to your book

I love shiny objects. I will literally buy one book over another because the cover is sexier.

While I'm probably just an outlier, the cover image definitely will affect your sales. When your book is shown on Amazon's website, before people click on it, it will be next to a lot of other books (whether it's in the search results, the "customers also bought" section, or elsewhere).

The only information people have on which to base their decisions about which books to click on is your title and your cover image (and your reviews, but we'll get to that later). Whether they realize it or not, these two factors directly dictate whether or not they'll click on your book, and in the end, whether they'll even have a chance to buy it.

And what makes a good cover?

It's tough to define exactly what makes a good cover – that's like try to explicitly detail what makes a good piece of art. However, I think I can boil it down to these three factors:

1. **It gets the point across**. By looking at your cover, someone should have an idea of what your book is about, and what benefit it offers.

2. **It's aesthetically pleasing**. Put simply: it looks good.

3. **It looks good as a small icon**. This is the kicker. On Amazon, people will almost always see just a very small version of your cover. This is because your book is usually going to be displayed in search results or the "customers also bought" section. This means that it shouldn't rely on small details to look good. The text and graphics should be large so that they can be identified even at small sizes.

Your task is to create a cover image. For this step, I highly recommend hiring someone unless your Photoshop skills are through the roof. Another option that I'm beginning to prefer (if you're proficient at Photoshop, but not a boss) is buying a stock photo or illustration, editing its dimensions, and adding the title yourself.

You can hire a freelancer by creating a fixed price project on eLance.com. Create a project, describing the idea you want to get across, the title, and the fact that it should look good at small resolutions. Give it a price ($100 should be enough to attract skilled artists). Next, prospective artists will enter their bids. Look over their portfolios and then hire one based on the quality and style of their previous work.

NOTE: The technical requirements for the cover image can be found at this link: **https://kdp.amazon.com/help?topicId=A2J0TRG6O PX0VM** (follow them or send them to your freelance artist)

The other option I mentioned was buying a stock photo off of a website like **http://www.canstockphoto.com** and then editing it slightly to transform it into a cover. This is cheaper than hiring someone, and you see exactly what you'll get. However, the options are limited.

This is the route I'm going for this book. It's the quickest and most efficient of the three options in my opinion.

NOTE: If you go this route, make sure you buy a large enough resolution (see Amazon's recommendations below) AND that you purchase the appropriate licensing option so that you can legally use it on an eBook you will sell.

Amazon's cover image suggestions (more info here): **https://kdp.amazon.com/help?topicId=A2J0TRG6OPX0VM**)

- A minimum of 625 pixels on the shortest side and 1000 pixels on the longest side

- For best quality, your image would be 2820 pixels on the shortest side and 4500 pixels on the longest side

Step 5: Write a blurb that will generate massive interest in your potential buyers

This is the final step of phase 3. You've come so far, young padawan.

Every book on Amazon has a blurb or a description. And so you must make yours.

Honestly, I'm not sure how much this impacts sales (I believe title, cover image, and reviews are more important), but it does play some role, so there's no reason to neglect it.

Most people make the mistake of simply describing their book, and what it's about. But as we covered before, you want to focus on the benefits. This is what will make your target reader stop and think "this book was written JUST FOR ME".

Over the past few years, I've befriended several copywriters, whose job is to produce sales letters that sell products. Their influence and advice has completely reshaped how I write these blurbs. If you go back and look at my descriptions for my earlier books, you'll see the difference.

Your task is to write a sales blurb that will be used for your book's description on Amazon. Follow this format:

ATTENTION GRABBING HEADLINE

Description

DESCRIPTIVE HEADLINE

- Benefits in bullet point form

To give you a concrete example, here's what I wrote for the blurb of this book. Pay close attention, because apparently it worked on you (cue evil scientist laugh):

HOW AN EXPERIMENT IN SELF-PUBLISHING QUICKLY TURNED INTO THOUSANDS OF DOLLARS IN MY POCKET EVERY WEEK (without spending a single cent)

I never considered myself an author… or even a good writer… But I did have aspirations of entrepreneurship and passive income…

All of us have knowledge and experiences that are invaluable to other people who are facing the problems and challenges we overcame yesterday.

Maybe it's how to build muscle. Maybe it's how to win in online poker. Maybe it's how to effectively use a particular application, like Evernote or Tinder. Maybe it's how to deal with intense social anxiety.

Whatever it is, we've all figured SOMETHING out...

...and the best part is this: people are MORE THAN WILLING TO PAY for information that solves their problems. The eBook market has EXPLODED and you can use your existing knowledge to cash in, just like I have.

That's why I created...

A Step-By-Step Blueprint That Shows You Exactly How To Determine Your Most Valuable Information, Write A Compelling Kindle eBook About It, Publish It On Amazon, And Most Importantly: Actually GUARANTEE SALES And Revenue

The book is organized into the following phases:

* Phase 1: How To Discover Your Most Profitable, Marketable Existing Knowledge

* Phase 2: A Simple System For Writing Easy-To-Follow, Engaging Books That Sell (without being a "good" writer)

* Phase 3: The 5 Things You Must Do Before Publishing To Ensure Maximum Sales

* Phase 4: A Step By Step Guide To Formatting, Uploading, And Publishing Your eBook (and cracking the key options that will determine your sales success)

* Phase 5: The Secret To Unleashing Amazon's Built-In Marketing Machine To Sell Thousands Of Copies

* BONUS: How To Maintain Sales In The Long Run, Build A Business Around Self-Publishing, And Other Common Questions Answered

Phase 4: A Step By Step Guide To Formatting, Uploading, And Publishing Your eBook (and cracking the key options that will determine your sales success)

WARNING: This chapter is not super fun. Don't expect a big celebration party. The good news is that it doesn't take much time. You can easily complete the following steps and make your book available in the Kindle store within an hour.

The first time I went to publish a book, I was confused. Amazon's publishing process is straightforward, but there were options that I couldn't quite understand how to utilize effectively. I knew what I was selecting – my book's category or search keywords, for example – but I didn't know what to choose so that people would actually be more likely to buy my book.

As I published book after book, I researched and experimented with different strategies for exploiting these options. Some immediately improved sales, other didn't. And so I continued to experiment.

I'm sure that my method could still use some fine tuning, but what you'll find on the following pages will surely give your book a step or three up on the competition that simply publish their book without keeping a keen eye on how the smaller options affect their success.

I will guide you through the overall process, pointing out the not-so-obvious things that should be done to optimize your book and its potential sales. However, Amazon's online help does a better job than I can do of detailing the minutiae of the process, so I suggest you reference that when you have questions about a specific option or step as we proceed.

You can find it here: **https://kdp.amazon.com/help**

Step 1: Finalize your book's format and make it ready to upload to Amazon

Uploading my first book was a disaster. It looked like a kindergarten student's attempt at self-publishing. The formatting was sloppy as hell.

The good news is that if you followed my previous formatting tips as you built your book, then this step will only take a matter of seconds.

Before you save your Word document, confirm that each of the following requirements is accounted for:

1. There is a page break in between every chapter (or between pages that should be separated by page turns) in your book (see Phase 2, Step 4 for more info).

2. You've included the following pages: title, copyright, contents, call to action for reviews, call to action to join your email list, about the author, and OPTIONALLY, your other books and a call to action to purchase another product (see Phase 3, Step 2 for more info).

3. Your table of contents is updated (see Phase 3, Step 2 for more info).

4. You've included bookmarks for the start and table of contents (see Phase 3, Step 2 for more info).

Once you check each of these items off your list, all you need to do is save your book as an HTML file. Select **File>Save As** and then choose **Webpage, filtered (*.htm, *.html)** from the **Save as type** dropdown menu in Word.

NOTE: If there are photos in your book, Word will save a folder along with your HTML file (e.g. if your html file is called **TITLE.HTML,** then the folder will be called **TITLE_files**). This folder will contain the image files that are referenced in the HTML file. In this case, you will have to compress the html file and the folder into a single ZIP file before uploading it to Amazon.

Step 2: Register for KDP (Kindle Direct Publishing) and begin the upload and publication process

Below is a step by step process to getting your book uploaded and published. I'll focus on the options that aren't obvious BUT have a large impact on your book's potential sales.

1. Register an account on **https://kdp.amazon.com/** (you can use your existing Amazon.com account here).

2. Navigate to your **Bookshelf** and click **Add New Title.**

3. Opt in for **KDP Select** at the top of the page. This will allow your book to be downloaded for free by Amazon Prime members (they get one free download per month). These downloads 'count' as sales in the sense that they boost your sales ranking, so I believe it's favorable to enroll new books in the program. The enrollment lasts 3 months, so if your book's selling well by the end of your enrollment term you can always opt out.

4. Fill in the title, subtitle, and description (a.k.a. Blurb) of your book in the appropriate boxes.

(**NOTE:** you can use basic html for the description to bold your headlines and italicize any relevant text. Use **BOLDED TEXT HERE** to bold text and <i>*ITALICIZED TEXT HERE*</i> to italicize text.)

6. Under **Verify Your Publishing Rights**, select **this is not a public domain work and I hold the necessary publishing rights** (assuming that you indeed did not copy other people's work in your book).

7. Under **Target Your Book To Customers**, select two categories into which to place your book using the following methodology to ensure maximum visibility inside Amazon's Kindle store:

    a. Navigate to Amazon's Kindle Bestseller lists: **http://www.amazon.com/Best-Sellers-Kindle-Store-eBooks/zgbs/digital-text/154606011/**

    b. Click on every category that your book could be placed into (expand the categories as far as possible – for example: **Non Fiction>Self Help>Creativity** as opposed to **Non Fiction** or **Self Help**), click on the 20th bestselling book on that list, and record its **Amazon Bestseller's Rank** under **Product Details**

c. Choose the two categories that have the highest number for this value (these are the least competitive categories, and will give your book the best chance of breaking into the first page of bestsellers and enjoying vastly increased visibility, and therefore sales)

8. Under **Target Your Book To Customers**, select seven keywords for your book using this methodology to ensure maximum visibility among Amazon's search results. Similarly to how I described how to test your potential ideas using Amazon's search auto-fill in Phase 1, you will do the same here:

a. In Amazon.com's search box, start typing in search terms that someone looking for a book similar to yours might use (AND that isn't already part of your title, subtitle, or description – these are automatically indexed)

b. If Amazon suggest something that makes sense as you begin typing, add this as a keyword (a keyword can be multiple words).

Returning to my *how to meet women during the day* book idea, here are two keywords I may choose:

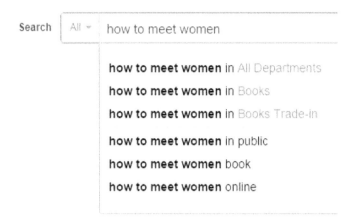

How to meet women in public

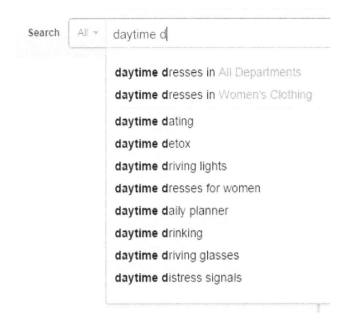

Or *daytime dating*

    c. Do this until you have seven keywords (separated by commas)

9. Upload your cover image file and HTML or ZIP file for your book and use Amazon's preview tool to scroll through the book and make sure the basic formatting looks right (pages are separated, images are displayed, etc.).

10. Click **Save and continue** to advance to pricing options.

11. You can edit this section at any point in the future to change your price (which we'll explore in Phase 5), but for now start by selecting **worldwide rights** under **Verify your publishing rights** (to make it available in all of Amazon's stores worldwide).

12. Under **KDP Pricing and Royalty**, set your price. For the first week or two, I suggest selecting **35% Royalty** and setting the price to **$0.99** (and setting the price for all other regions automatically).

NOTE: You'll change this to 70% and a higher price soon, but starting the book at 99 cents is a favorable way to launch the book as we'll explore in Phase 5.

13. Accept Amazon KDP's Terms and Conditions and click **Save and publish**…

…your book will be available for purchase in a matter of hours. CONGRATULATIONS.

Phase 5: The Secret To Unleashing Amazon's Built-In Marketing Machine To Sell Thousands Of Copies

If you did everything up until this point, you now have a book published in the Amazon Kindle store. But if you stop now, you might not even make a single dime.

In the end, this section of the course, marketing your eBook, is what will have the biggest impact on your financial success. And most people who self-publish don't like marketing. They're creative types who like to write, not sell.

By putting in work now, after your book's been published, you'll put yourself in a good position to rise far above the average self-published author and actually make some decent revenue off of your work.

But MAKE NO MISTAKE: don't treat this section as an afterthought. Put in quality, focused work here so that you can walk away from this project knowing that you left it all on the floor. So that you can rest easy knowing that you did sufficient work in creating, publishing, AND marketing your book. Otherwise you essentially "wasted" all the time you just put into creating and publishing your book.

On the next few pages I'll lay out a straightforward plan for you to follow in order to get Amazon selling your book for you – this is the reason that you're publishing on Kindle in the first place. It's going to take some work up front, but the beauty is that Amazon will quickly take over and sell for you if you execute this method properly.

This method is the number one reason my books tend to sell better and better with each successive release: my attention to and knowledge of Amazon's marketing system has evolved over time. Take advantage of my knowledge and experience and make yourself some money.

Step 1: Understand how Amazon selects which books to promote

Amazon is an amazingly efficient website: it knows how to sell, especially when it comes to Kindle books, where impulse buys are the norm.

Someone who's scrolling or searching through Kindle books is likely a consumer of them. So what does Amazon do? It fills up all of the available real estate on your screen, from the sidebar to the *Customers Who Bought This Item Also Bought* section with links to books similar to those that you're looking at now, ones you've looked at in the past, or ones you've purchased and bought in the past.

It presents you with an incredible number of options that are extremely relevant to your interests. And when this happens, you're likely to purchase something. And purchasers of books – Kindle eBooks in particular – tend to buy A LOT of them.

I probably have bought ten books for my Kindle that I haven't even begun to read yet.

So the question is, how does Amazon choose WHICH relevant books to display, and – MORE IMPORTANTLY – how can you make sure that Amazon chooses your book over something similar.

The truth is that Amazon does what's most profitable. It chooses books that SELL WELL and that are WELL REVIEWED (i.e. it chooses objectively *GOOD* books, proven to sell). So the big secret to taking advantage of Amazon's built in marketing system is to sell a lot of books and to get a lot of good reviews. Sounds easy, right?

If you get your book to sell a bunch of copies up front and get a decent amount of solid reviews, Amazon will take over and begin to sell for you.

Now that you're armed with this powerful yet kind of obvious information, let's explore my method for accomplishing both of these goals without spending a single penny on advertising.

Step 2: Get one or two reviews posted for your book to get it out of "no man's land"

Let's be honest: NO ONE is going to buy a book that has ZERO reviews. It's not worth the risk.

You wouldn't do it, and neither would I. We can't expect random Amazon visitors to give it a chance either.

So your first step is to get one or two reviews to keep appearances up. For this step I usually email a PDF version of my book to any friends and family that I think would be interested in the book and request a timely review.

Is this dishonest? No, I don't think so. It's a necessary step to bypass the insurmountable discrimination that a self-published author whose book has zero reviews faces. I also expect the people to whom I email the book to actually read it; this way their review actually offers value by offering a unique perspective on the book.

Look at it this way: even if you get three of four great reviews from friends and family BUT your book sucks, you'll quickly aggregate enough negative reviews to offset this and your below average book won't sell in the long run.

Step 3: Discount your book for a "promotional period" and announce it anywhere and everywhere that you can think of

Here's where the hard work comes in. And here's where I can't hold your hand and offer an exact prescription for what you must do. You have to step up and bring your A game.

I currently have the benefit of possessing a decently sized email list from my blog. When I release a book, I send several emails to them, and a number of them inevitably buy it. That's why I strongly suggest capturing the emails of people who buy your books: it will pay you back tenfold in the future.

The more times you go through this process, the more success you'll have because you'll have a greater amount of potential buyers who already like your work to reach out to. But you can certainly succeed your very first time as well, if you put in the effort and follow these steps.

__Your task is to price your book at $0.99 and promote it in every relevant place that you can think of. Below are my top suggestions.__

NOTE: Why $0.99? Why not free? The fact is that yes, more people will download your book if you make it free. However, people don't value what they don't pay for, even if it's just a dollar. They probably won't even read it. If they do, great, but realize that freeloaders are more likely to leave a bad review, because they haven't invested anything (and they probably rarely do).

MOST IMPORTANTLY, free "sales" don't improve your book's sales rank inside of Amazon because free books operate within their own rank. The moment you make it "for-pay" again, it will immediately drop to the bottom of the rankings.

Use these places to promote it, and think of your own as well:

1. Facebook: Announce to your friends that you just published a book and request that they support you and buy it for a single dollar (and leave you a review).

2. Online communities: Large groups of enthusiasts come together on internet forums (i.e. Reddit or specific forums like Bodybuiling.com). Post a thread announcing your book's promotional period. These people often love to support other community members.

3. Bloggers: Send an email to bloggers who run blogs about topics relevant to your book. Just be straightforward and tell them you just published a book that their readers might find helpful and send them a free PDF copy for them to peruse. If they like it, they'll post a review or email their list for you. Don't be intimidated here: email as many of them as you can find – the worst that will happen is that they won't respond.

4. Local newspapers and television outlets: News people are always looking for a story. The fact that a local person just self-published a book and that there is a "promotional period" can definitely be enough to get a quick blurb written up. My friend was just interviewed on the local news because of a book he published, so don't think this is outside of your reach.

Be CREATIVE and RESILIENT here. No option is too silly to pursue. Exhaust any and all possibilities that you can think of, even if you don't think that they'll work. In the end, even a small boost in initial sales and reviews will be enough for Amazon to sell some copies for you.

NOTE: After the promotional period has ended, you should edit your book on KDP, change your royalty option to 70%, and up the price to something in between $2.99 and $9.99. This is the price range that you're allowed to use for the 70% royalty option. For a longer book (150+ pages) I suggest starting the price at $9.99, for an Intermediate book (100+ pages) I suggest $4.99, and for a short book (<100 pages) I suggest $2.99. This is only a rough guide: make a choice and give it a few weeks at that price point, you can always adjust it after.

How To Maintain Sales In The Long Run, Build A Business Around Self-Publishing, And Other Common Questions Answered

The potential profits that Amazon offers us via Kindle publishing are amazing. It's truly changed my life: both financially and otherwise. That's why I wrote this book – I firmly believe that it's a process that anyone can follow to achieve similar, if not better, results.

If you pick up the pen as I have and begin, as I also have, to explore your interests on a deeper level, you'll also undoubtedly come away with a deeper knowledge of yourself. When you're in the flow of writing, it's like some part of your brain turns on that's normally dormant: you awaken some part of you that allows you to express yourself on a whole different level.

Once you build the habit of writing, it becomes an invaluable tool in your life. Your grasp of language and words increases tenfold, and you're able to express yourself on a higher, more accurate level as a result.

This works internally and externally, meaning through your own internal thought patterns and through your conversations with others. You can better analyze your own thoughts and experiences, and you can communicate more effectively with others.

This book, up until this point, has illustrated exactly how to publish a book on Kindle and give it a solid chance at accumulating sales. But even after you hit publish and market the book to your audience, there are many more relevant options and questions that arise.

In this final chapter of the book, I'll attempt to aggregate the answers that I found most useful as I began to turn Kindle publishing into a long term business venture. More importantly, I'll provide you with questions that you might not even think of, but that are essential to long term profit and success.

Should I publish a paperback version of my book?

This is undoubtedly the first question you will face after publishing a Kindle eBook. My answer: yes, definitely, given that you have some extra time to spare.

The reasons I advocate publishing a paperback along with your eBook are:

1. It's badass to have physical copies of your own book laying around your place.

2. It makes your eBook look more legitimate when people see that it also has a paperback version, making them more likely to buy the eBook version. Something that's just an eBook seems less official.

3. It generates some extra profit. I don't make close to as much off of my paperback books as the Kindle versions, but I still do make a considerable amount of money.

I'm not going to get into the specifics of paperback publishing, but it's super easy to do using Amazon's Createspace service:
https://www.createspace.com/

The formatting and uploading are actually easier than with Kindle – the only thing that's tricky is the cover image and getting it to wrap correctly. If your book is short (about 100 pages or less), you may not be able to fit your name and title on the spine of the book (and that's what can cause an issue).

Should I create an author page on Amazon?

Amazon offers a service called Author Central that allows you to create an Amazon webpage that serves as a place to display your books, your biography, your blog, and your photo, among other things.

You can check mine out here: **http://www.amazon.com/David-De-Las-Morenas/e/B00AUMAVMA/**

Honestly, I believe that you might as well create an Author page if you took the time to publish a book. I don't know if it will improve your sales if you don't have multiple books on Amazon, but surely it can't hurt.

Its most useful feature is probably allowing you to edit your books description after publishing, without having to go through the entire approval process again (doing it though KDP where you initially published the book).

To create an Author's page for yourself:

1. Register an account here: **https://authorcentral.amazon.com/** (you can use your existing Amazon.com account)

2. Search for your books to link them to your new page

3. Upload a photo, add your blog, add a brief biography, and add any other information you choose

NOTE: This page seems to rank well with Google, so it's the first thing people see if they Google my name. I think this is awesome, but you may prefer to stay anonymous. Although I assume you're using a pen name if this is the case.

Should I use Amazon affiliate links to sell my eBook?

Amazon offers a service called Amazon Associates. By registering an account there it allows you to create links to specific products on Amazon that, when people click on them to buy products, award you a small commission (around 3-7% on average).

The beauty of this system is that when they click your link, a cookie is stored in their internet browser for 24 hours. You also make a commission off of anything they buy on Amazon, not just the product you linked to.

This means that if anyone clicks one of your links and then buys anything on Amazon in the next 24 hours, you make a small commission.

What this means for you: when you're marketing your eBook you're going to be providing people with links to buy your book on Amazon. If you provide them with an affiliate link, rather than a basic link, you'll make some extra cash in the long run.

And if you run a blog, you can use Amazon affiliate links every time you mention a product in one of your articles.

What I make from this program isn't much, but it is something. And, as I think you can see by now, stacking revenue sources (Kindle, paperback, affiliate income, etc.) is the magic that allows me to make a good income from Amazon.

You can register an account here: **https://affiliate-program.amazon.com/** (again, you can use your existing Amazon account)

What can I do if my sales drop off sometime in the future?

If you successfully launched your eBook using this manual, then Amazon should take care of sellIng It for a while. However, in the long run there tends to be a point when sales drop off a bit. This can be due to poor reviews or just a natural drop in sales.

When this happens you can sit there, sulk, and accept this fate OR you can man up and take action to get your book back on the bestsellers list. For me, this is tough, because I'm often working on a new book and I don't feel like taking the time and energy to rejuvenate old ones, but from time to time I still do it.

To reignite your sales, you must follow the exact same steps you used to jumpstart them in the first place: drop the price to $0.99 for a week and then PROMOTE, PROMOTE, PROMOTE. This will boost your sales and reviews: there is no magic here, just basic logic.

Here is the result of a recent promotion I did for my book "Dominate" to resurrect its sales (number 1 on the Men's Health Bestseller list within hours):

How do I report my new income on my taxes?

By far the worst thing about making money on Amazon as we've explored so far is doing your taxes. Amazon will send you **1099-MISC** forms for all of the profits they've paid you and you must report these earnings to the IRS (or whatever your governing tax body is).

I don't have the authority to tell you exactly how to deal with these taxes but here are a few basic guidelines:

1. This income is classified as self-employment income and must be reported as such. Unfortunately, this means you'll pay extra taxes on your profits (versus traditional income from an employer).

2. Amazon doesn't take anything out for taxes as they pay you (e.g. social security), so you'll be giving a sizeable chunk of your revenue back.

3. Because it's self-employment income, you can report any related expenses (cover design, proof reading, advertising, etc.). You only pay taxes on your profits (revenue MINUS costs), so be sure to report all related expenses.

4. You'll likely get multiple 1099-MISC forms from Amazon (separate for US sales, Worldwide sales, Createspace sales, Amazon associate earnings, etc.). The good news is they can all be aggregated and grouped together, since they are all part of your "book business".

How do I create an entire business that revolves around self-publishing books on Amazon?

If you're really pumped about this whole process, the good news is that you can definitely build a profitable business around it. As I've hinted throughout, this is exactly what I've done. Despite having two other "jobs", my main income stream comes from Amazon.

While I'm sure there are infinite ways you could structure such a business, the following is what worked for me. I'm going to breeze through this and offer only a basic outline, because detailing this process could easily be an entire book or two of its own.

1. Create a blog that focuses on a particular niche

There are a lot of good guides out there on how to start a blog, but you'll want to buy a domain name, a hosting package, and install WordPress on your site. Then you'll want to make it look pretty (or hire someone else to).

The most important thing here is that you choose a particular niche that you can write a collection of books around. This will attract readers and followers who will likely consume and purchase a lot of your content. My niche is men's health and self-improvement. Some other popular niches are fitness, habits, email marketing, and dating (things that there's a near-infinite demand for).

2. Create an email list

We went over this in *Phase 3, Step 2*. You must build an email list. It's the most effective way to stay in touch with and sell to your audience. Things like Facebook, Twitter, and Instagram are good ways to connect and build interest, but email is king. Any of those services could shut down or shut down your account at any moment. Emails are forever, and people actually tend to read them.

3. Capture the emails of your book buyers and blog readers

Also, as explored in *Phase 3, Step 2*, you should include an enticing offer like a free eBook to motivate people to sign up for your list. Basically this means that when someone signs up for your list, you email them or link them to a PDF file. You should include a call to action to sign up for your list at the beginning of your books as well as throughout your blog.

4. Publish books

This is obvious. You need to give your followers a way to pay you for your valuable information. This is what this book just taught you.

5. Write several articles on your blog relevant to each book you publish

While most of your sales will come from Amazon and your initial marketing efforts, writing two or three articles on each book you publish will supply some flow of traffic to your books. More importantly, it gives you something to write about. I've gotten to the point where I only publish one or two articles a month. But I try to make them super valuable – and structure them so they sell a few books.

6. Create a higher priced item that you sell on your own

You want to give your followers and readers something that they can buy if they want more than a book. The possibilities here are endless from online courses to coaching. I offer an online course. You can check it out by looking a few pages ahead (and this is where you should include yours as well: at the end of your book – as well as on your blog, of course).

7. Practice strong email marketing

You need to engage your readership to build a relationship with them. This is one of my main focuses right now. My basic strategy is trying to email once or twice a week with valuable content or tips, so that when I release a book they trust me and know that it's likely to be valuable as well.

There are a lot of good blogs dedicated to mastering this subject, so I recommend doing more research of your own.

And that wraps it up. Amazon truly presents an incredible opportunity if you embrace it and capitalize on its strengths. I wish you the best of luck in your journey, and feel free to contact me on my blog if you have any questions:
http://www.HowToBeast.com

Can You Do Me a Favor?

Thank you for buying and reading my book. I'm confident that you're well on your way to making good money off of your existing knowledge if you simply follow the steps I've laid out here.

Before you go, I have a small favor to ask. Would you take a minute to write a brief blurb about this book on Amazon? Reviews are the best way for independent authors (like me) to get noticed and sell more books. I also read every review and use the feedback to write future revisions – and future books, even.

Thank you.

You Might Also Like My New Online Bootcamp

If you liked this book, I believe you'll find my online course *28 Days to Alpha* invaluable.

It's **An Easy to Follow System I Developed That Took Me from an Insecure, Lonely "Beta Male" To a Fearless, Dominant Man.**

This online course is **An Accelerated Bootcamp That Will Teach You How to Develop a Dominant Presence, Effortlessly Approach Women, Discover Your Primary Masculine Purpose, And Become an All Around "Alpha Male" Regardless Of Your Current Looks, Job, Or Sexual Confidence.**

I invite you to read more about the course here: **www.28DaysToAlpha.com**

My Other Books

If you enjoyed this book, you'll find my others awesome, too. They're all available on Amazon.

1. *Dominate: Conquer your fears. Become the man you want to be.*

2. *Shredded Beast: Get lean. Build muscle. Be a man.*

3. *The Book of Alpha: 30 Rules I Followed to Radically Enhance My Confidence, Charisma, Productivity, Success, and Life*

4. *The Book of Bulking: Workouts, Groceries, and Meals for Building Muscle*

5. *The Simple Art of Bodybuilding: A Practical Guide to Training and Nutrition*

About the Author

David De Las Morenas is an engineer, personal trainer, and internet entrepreneur known for his bestselling books on men's health and entrepreneurship.

You can follow him at: **www.HowToBeast.com**

CPSIA information can be obtained
at www.ICGtesting.com
Printed in the USA
LVHW081340070319
609844LV00033B/610/P